Salt and Pepper

over
1001
Shakers

With Prices

Larry Carey and
Sylvia Tompkins

Schiffer Publishing Ltd

77 Lower Valley Road, Atglen, PA 19310

Dedication

This book is dedicated to the many salt and pepper collectors who, through the years, have asked us "Why don't you do a book?", and most especially to Peter Schiffer, who pushed and persuaded us into finally doing it.

Acknowledgements

We greatly appreciate the encouragement and assistance of fellow collectors and especially the following contributors to this book:

Jeanne Fouts, Bob and Joyce Gentile, Marty Grossman, Lorraine Haywood, Phil Mays, Linda Nothnagel, Muriel O'Connor, Sandy Piggott, Judy Posner, Therrie Sherwood, Marcia Smith, Diane Thorn, Irene Thornburg, Ruth Wittlief and 'Tiques Auction.

We also wish to thank the staff of Schiffer Publishing for their expert assistance.

Title Page Photo: Boy sitting in watermelon slice. 5". Probably Japan. 1960s. $125-150.

All prices stated are for sets and measurements are for height (usually of tallest item), unless noted otherwise.

Copyright © 1994 by
Larry Carey and Sylvia Tompkins

Library of Congress Catalog Number: 94-65428

Printed in the United States of America.
ISBN: 0-88740-607-6

Published by Schiffer Publishing Ltd.
77 Lower Valley Road
Atglen, PA 19310
Please write for a free catalog.
This book may be purchased from the publisher.
Please include $2.95 postage.
Try your bookstore first.

Autographed copies may be ordered from the authors (Addresses inside front cover). Please include $2.95 postage.

Introduction

After it was finally determined that doing a book had become a reality, the first decision was the *subject matter*. As we plan a series of books, we decided to take a somewhat different approach from previous authors by having one major and two or three minor categories in each book. Primary coverage of this book is devoted to Black Americana, natives and related nationalities. Minor categories are cat characters, mermaids, and Niagara Falls. Although some sets have been included in previous books, we wished to make coverage of each category as comprehensive as possible. Further, we have illustrated comparisons of color, size and design variations not formerly shown. Values are based on our experience and input from contributors. They are intended as a guide only and will vary depending on condition, geographical area, knowledge of the seller or buyer, and to some extent, sheer luck! Subjects under consideration for future books include nodders, Disneyana, advertising, anthropomorphics and characters.

Collecting novelty salt and peppers is a fantastic hobby. Shakers are attractive, interesting, small, generally afford-able, offer an endless variety and provide a continual learning experience. Finding that special set is really great! But the best and most rewarding part of our hobby is the lifetime friends we've made.

Collect what you like, not just what may be "popular" at the moment. Don't overlook newer sets which are affordable today but may be expensive tomorrow, if you can find them! While shakering (marketing), don't be reluctant to ask the person buying shakers next to you, "Do you collect?" and "Do you know about the Club?" Membership in the Novelty Salt & Pepper Shakers Club offers the opportunity to contact well over 1000 other people who share the same affliction! You can trade, buy, sell or just chat about shakers to your heart's content. We think Mike Schneider in his "The Complete Salt and Pepper Shaker Book" said it best when he stated that if you want to buy his book "and also join the Club, but can't afford to do both, join the Club first. It will become your most important asset as a collector." For information about the Club, contact the authors.

Contents

Chefs with trays of fruit. 3.5" and 3.25". Japan. 1950s. Tall set, $45-50. Short set, $30-35.

Chef and maid, and chefs with knives. 3.25". Chef and maid, paper label Japan. 1960s. $60-70. Chefs with knives, Japan. Pre-1950. $75-85.

Waving chefs and maids. 2.5". Japan. 1950s. $40-45.

Chefs, and chef and maid. 3.25" and 2.5". Germany . Pre-WWII. $90-100.

Chefs and maids. 2.5" and 3". Japan. 1960s. $35-40.

Shopping couple. 3". Japan. Pre-1950. $75-85.

Cooks. 2.75". Paper label, Japan. 1960s. $50-60.

Chefs and maids. First row: Chefs have cleaver/knife in left hand. First set is a white-faced black. 3". Japan. 1950s/1960s. $25-35. Second row: Chefs and maids, each holding a spoon. 3". Japan. 1950s/1960s. $18-25. Third row: Chefs and maids with gold trim. 3".

First two sets, Japan; last set, Occupied Japan. 1940s/1950s. $30-40. Fourth row: Various chalkware, except last set which is a composition material. 2.5"-3". Probably U.S.A. 1950s. If in good condition, $15-25.

Chef and maid, "chocolate milk" faces. 4". Japan. Pre-1950s. $65-75.

Chef and maid. 3.5". Japan. Pre-1950. $75-85.

Chef and maid. 4.75". U.S.A. 1960s. $90-100.

Chefs and maids. 3". Set on left, Japan. 1950s. $75-85. Center , PY Japan. 1950s. $90-100. Set on right, private ceramicist. U.S.A. 1970s. $35-45.

Chef and maid. 3.5". Japan. 1960s. $55-60.

Chef and maid, heavy. 4.5". U.S.A. 1960s. $110-125.

Chef and maid. 4.5". Japan. Pre-1950. $65-75.

Chef and maid. 4.5". U.S.A. "Warranted 22 kt. gold."
1970s. $90-100.

Chefs and maids. 4.75". Set on left, Japan. 1950s. $65-75. Set on
right, probably U.S.A. 1960s. $55-65.

Chef and maid. Brown pottery. 5". Paper label,
Japan. 1960s. $85-100.

Chefs and maids. 4". Set on left, Japan. 1960s. $50-55. Set on right, probably U.S.A. 1960s. $60-65.

Chef and maid. 5". Private ceramicist. U.S.A. 1970s. Obviously a set, but incorrectly painted as 2 peppers. $50-60.

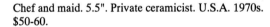

Chef and maid. 5.5". Private ceramicist. U.S.A. 1970s. $50-60.

Chefs and maids. 4.5". Private ceramicist. U.S.A. 1980s. Left set, $30-35. Right set, $45-50.

Chefs and maids, white-faced blacks. First row , 5". Probably U.S.A.
1960s. Sets, $65-75; single, $30-35. Second row; first set, 4". Japan.
1950s. $45-50. Second set, 4.5". Probably U.S.A. 1960s. $55-60.

Chef and maid. 5". Probably U.S.A. 1960s. $85-100.

Chef and maid. Brown pottery . 4.75". Paper label, Japan. 1960s.
$55-60.

Chefs and maids. 4.75". Probably U.S.A. 1960s. $45-50.

Chefs and maids. First row, 4"-4.5". First two sets, U.S.A. 1960s.
$35-40. Third set, Occupied Japan, late 1940s. $55-60. Second row:
3.75"-4". Japan. 1950s/1960s. $25-30. Third row: 4.25"-4.5".
Probably Japan. 1980s. $15-20.

Chefs and maids. First row: first set, 5". U.S.A. 1960s. $55-60.
Second set, 4.75". U.S.A. 1960s. $55-60. Third set, 4.25". U.S.A.
1960s. $45-50. Second row: 4.5". U.S.A. 1960s. $35-40. Third row:
first two sets, 4.5". Japan. Pre-1950. $40-45. Third set, 4". Japan. Pre-
1950. $38-40.

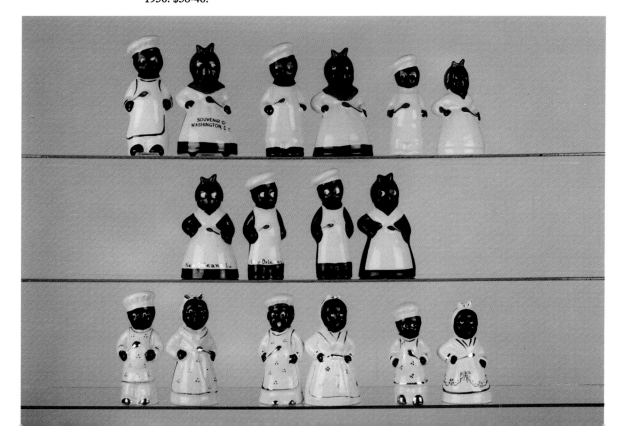

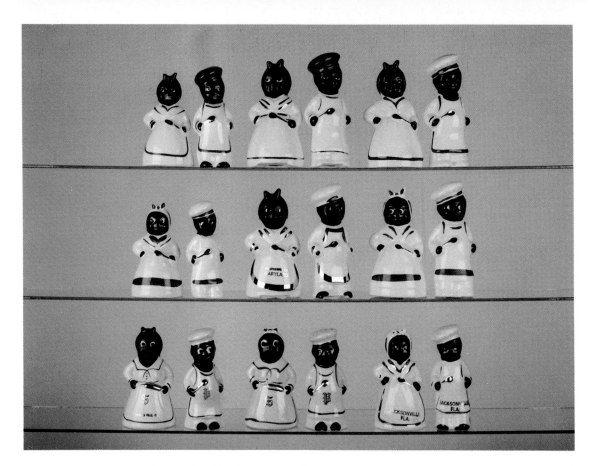

Chefs and maids. First row, 4.5"-5". Probably U.S.A. 1960s. First set, $45-50. Second and third sets, $55-60. Second row , 4.25"-5". Probably U.S.A. 1960s. First set, $45-50. Second and third sets, $55-60. Third row: 4.25"-4.5". First and second sets, Holley Ross China. 1960s. $55-60. Third set, probably U.S.A. 1960s. $45-50.

Chefs and maids. First row: 4". Japan. 1950s. $35-40. Second row: 4.5". Possibly U.S.A. 1960s. $45-50. Third row: 4"-4.25". First two sets probably U.S.A. 1960s. $35-40. Third set, Japan. Pre-1950. $40-45.

Chefs and maids. First row 4.25". U.S.A. 1960s. $65-75. Second row: first set, 3.75". Occupied Japan. Late 1940s. $60-65. Second and third sets, 4.5". Japan. 1950s. $60-65.

Chefs and maids. 4.5". Probably U.S.A. 1960s. $55-65.

Chef and maid. 4.5". Paper label, Japan. 1960s. $75-90.

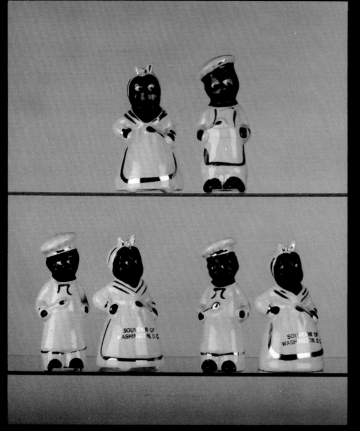

Chefs and maids. First row, 5.25". Darker yellow than sets on second row. Second row, 4.75". All sets, U.S.A. 1960s. $55-60.

Chefs and maids. Pink is hard to find. First row: 4.5". Probably U.S.A. 1960s. $75-85. Second row: first set 4.5". U.S.A. 1960s. $75-85. Second set 5". U.S.A. 1960s. $65-75.

Chefs and maids. First row, 4.5"-4.75". Probably U.S.A. 1960s. $55-60. Second row, 5". Probably U.S.A. 1960s. $60-65. Third row, 4.5"-5". Probably U.S.A. 1960s. First set, $50-55. Second set, $40-45.

Chefs and maids. Gray is very hard to find. First row , 5". U.S.A. 1960s. $90-100. Second row: first set, 5". U.S.A. 1960s. $90-100. Second set, 4.25". U.S.A. 1960s. $65-75.

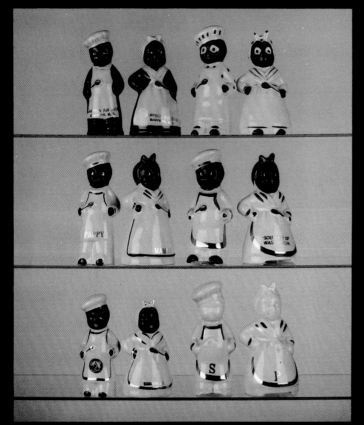

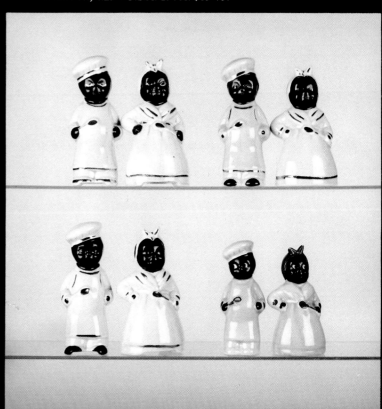

Chefs and maids. 5", U.S.A. 1960s. $55-60. Note differences in shade and gold trim.

Chefs and maids. 6.75"-7". Probably U.S.A. 1960s. $75-85.

Chefs and maids. 4.75"-5". Probably U.S.A. 1960s. $55-60.

Chefs and maids. First and second rows, 5.75". U.S.A. 1950s. Set, $90-100; single, $45-50. Third row, 5.25". First set probably U.S.A. 1950s. $75-80. Second set, private ceramicist. U.S.A. 1960s. $45-50.

Chef and maid. 7". Probably U.S.A. 1960s. $90-100.

Chefs and maids. 5". Probably U.S.A. 1960s. $75-85.

Chef and maid. Brown pottery. 4.75" and 4". Japan. 1960s. Tall, $65-70. Short, $55-60.

Unpainted chef and maid. 5.5". Probably U.S.A. 1960s. $75-85.

Chefs and maids. 7-7.5", private ceramicists. 1980s. $50-60.

Various sizes of chefs and maids in red, white, and blue with blue polka dots on scarf. All paper label, Japan. 1960s. First row: 6", 8", 5". $75-85, $110-125, $55-60. Second row: 5", 2.75", 6". $55-60, $40-45, $200+.

Chef and maid. 6.5". Japan. Pre-1950. If in good condition, $125-150.

Chef and maid, with stove mustard on tray. S&P 4.25", on tray 4.75". Japan. 1960s. $150-175. Larger matching salt and pepper, 4.75". Japan. 1960s. $65-75.

Chef and maid with stove grease jar, produced in many colors. 5.25", stove 4.75". U.S.A. 1960s. $225-250.

Chef and maid with stove grease jar, red clay pottery. 4.5". Japan. 1960s. If in good condition, $175-200.

Chef and maid with log cabin grease jar. 4.75", cabin 4.25". U.S.A. 1960s. $250-275.

Chef and maid with log cabin grease jar. 7". Cabin 4.25". U.S.A. 1960s. $300+.

Chef and maid heads that fit into spoon rest tray formed by arms and hands. 3.25". Paper label, Japan. 1960s. $150-175.

Chef and maid heads on spoon rest tray formed by arms and hands. 4" tall, 6.75" long. U.S.A. 1960s. $125-150.

Chef and maid. Composition material. 6". Probably U.S.A. 1960s. $90-100.

Butler and maid. 5.5". Brayton Laguna. 1950s. If in good condition,
$250. Lower shelf shows 3 styles of Brayton shaker bottoms.

Chefs and maids. 5.5". Brayton's Studio, Laguna Beach, CA
(Brayton Laguna). 1950s. If in good condition, $90-100.

Couple. 5.5". Brayton Laguna. 1950s. $100-125.

Men with turbans. S&P on each end. 4". No mark. 1950s. Figurine and planter in center stamped Riddell, California, which was taken over by Brayton Laguna. $250+.

Chefs and maids. 7". Metlox Pottery of California. 1980s. Company ceased business June, 1989. Issue price, $35; current value, $150-200.

Salty and Peppy. 7.75" and 4.5". Pearl China. U.S.A. 1960s. Large set, $200-250. Small set, $125-150.

Chef with spoon, maid with dish. 6.25". Lefton, Japan. 1960s. $175-200.

Chef and assistant. 5". Japan. 1950s. $175-200.

Single chef pepper. 5". Probably U.S.A. 1960s. $65-75.

Stacking chef condiment. 5.5". Japan. 1960s. $125-150.

Single chef. 5.5". Paper label, Japan. 1960s. $25.

Single chef. 5". Possibly U.S.A. 1960s. $40-50.

Black and French chefs. 4.75"-5". Chefs on fishbone tray , California,
U.S.A. 1960s. $75-100. Set on left marked Grimes, California.
U.S.A. 1960s. $65-75. Set on right distributed by Sarsaparilla Deco
Designs, NJ. 1990s. $15-18.

Chefs condiment. 4". Germany. Pre-WWII. $350+.

"Cream of Wheat" chefs. 5". Japan. 1960s. $125-150.

Waiter holding beer mugs condiment. 4.25". Probably Japan. 1960s.
$300+.

Chef with barrels condiment on left. 5.5" Probably Japan. 1960s. $150-175. On right, waiter with barrels condiment. 4.25". Japan. 1960s. $175-200.

Lady with barrels condiment. 5.5". Fairyland China, Japan. 1960s. $125-140.

"Chief Coffee Maker". 5". Probably Japan. 1960s. If proper set, $175-200.

White chef holding black cat; black chef holding chicken. 4.5".
Shefford (not Shafford), Japan. 1950s. $110-125. Smaller set, 3.5".
Japan. 1950s. $40-50.

Chefs. 6.25". Probably Japan. 1960s. If in good condition, $75-85.

Chefs with bottles and knives. 3.25" Probably Japan.
1960s. $75-85.

Waiters carrying bottles. 4.75". Probably Japan. 1960s. $200+.

Partial chef and maid spice set. 3". Japan. 1960s. If complete six-piece set, $90-100.

Chef and maid canisters. 3". Japan. Pre-1950. $60-70.

Salty and Peppy. Native chefs. 5.25". Wales, Japan. 1960s. $65-75.

Chefs. 5.5". Maker unknown. 1960s. If in good condition, $40-50.

Maid with square-shaped pots. 5.5". Paper label, Japan. 1960s. $200-225.

Maid holding pots. 4.75". Maker unknown. 1960s. If in good condition, $225-250.

Chef and maid servers. 5.25". Japan. 1960s. $150-200.

Chef and maid. 5.5". U.S.A. 1960s. $225-250.

The Turtleneck Couple. 4.75". Probably Japan. 1960s. Has matching oil and vinegar. S&P, $100-125.

Chef and maids carrying baskets and buckets. 4.75". Paper label, Japan. 1960s. Left and center sets, $85-100. Right set, $115-125.

"Dinah's Shack, Palo Alto, California". 2.75". Japan. Pre-1950. $110-125.

Ladies in yellow dresses. 3.25". Germany . Pre-WWII. Shaker on right incised no. 6110. Possibly 2 singles. $100 each.

Butlers and maids. First row: 5", 6", 4.75". Japan. 1950s. $90-100, $125-140, $90-100. Second row, 4.25"-4.5". First two sets, U.S.A. 1960s. $75-85. Third and fourth sets, Japan. 1950s. $90-100.

Maids. 6.5". Probably U.S.A. 1960s. If in good condition, set $75-90, single $35-40.

Three-maids, looking for mates. Center maid marked "Little Switzerland of Ohio." 4.5". Left and center: probably U.S.A. Right: Japan. 1960s. Center: $40-50. Left and right: $25-30.

Deco chef and maid. 4". Western Germany. 1960s. $90-100.

Aunt Jemimas. 3". Elbee Art of Ohio. 1960s. If in good condition, $45-50.

Chef and maid busts with flat backs. 4.25". Japan. 1960s. $150-175.

Cute children. 3". G Novelty Co., Japan. 1960s. $150-175.

Chef and maid heads. First and second rows: 3"-3.5". U.S.A. private ceramicist. 1980s. $20-25. Third row, 3". Japan. Pre-1950. First set, if in good condition, $110-125. Second set, $60-70.

Chef and maid heads. 2.5". Japan. 1950s. $50-60.

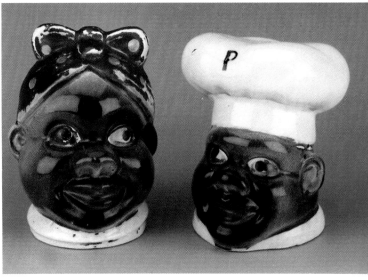

Chef and maid heads. 3.5". Japan. 1950s. If in good condition, $90-100.

Singers. 3". Probably U.S.A. 1960s. $65-75.

Ladies heads. 2". Probably U.S.A. 1950s. Eyes are shaker holes. $50-60.

Busts, chalkware or composition material. 3.5". U.S.A. 1950s. $60-75.

Couples, he is smoking pipe. Set on left, 4.25". Japan. 1950s. $100-110. Set on right with jiggly eyes. 4.5". Marked Empress, Japan. If in good condition, $100-110.

Gardening couples. 3.5". Enesco, Japan. 1960s. $80-100.

The Valentine couples. Left set, 5". Japan. 1950s. Right set, 4.75". Shafford, Japan. 1950s. $150-175.

Children sitting in nut shell dish. 3". Poinsettia Studios, CA. Probably 1960s. $100-125. Set on right is Japan copy , 2.75". $50-60.

Children holding corn. 3". Japan. 1960s. $150-175.

Band condiment. 3". Germany. Pre-WWII. $300+.

Man pushing S&P children in pram condiment. 3.5". Germany. Pre-WWII. Extremely rare. $500+.

Ladies with melons condiments. 4" and 3.75". Germany. Pre-WWII. $250+.

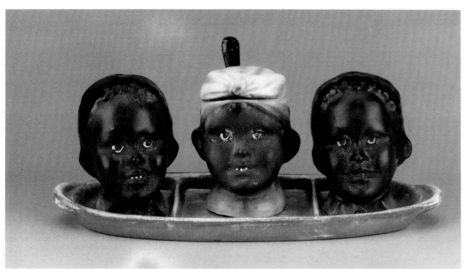

Heads on tray condiment. 2". Germany . Pre-WWII. $250-300.

Fisherman open salt and pepper. 5.5". Japan. 1960s. $200+.

"A Nod to Abe". 5.5". The 1991 S&P Club Convention set, designed by Betty Harrington, the primary designer for Ceramic Arts Studio, Madison, WI. Set on left is marked #1 and signed by Betty Harrington. Set on right was available to S&P Club members. 400 sets were produced by Regal China Corp., who ceased business in June 1992. The #1 set sold at the Club Convention Auction for $1100. The set on right originally sold for $35, current value $150-200.

Bottom of #1 set.

Removable hat as a cover

Betty Harrington

Turnabout couple. 5". Paper label, Japan. 1960s. $175-200.

Reverse side of turnabout couple.

Made for each other. Composition material. U.S.A. 1980s. $75-90.

Tap dancers. 5". Paper label, Japan. 1960s. $110-125.

Indians. 4.5". Japan. 1960s. $75-85.

Ladies with brooms. 4.25". Norcrest, Japan. 1960s. $150-175.

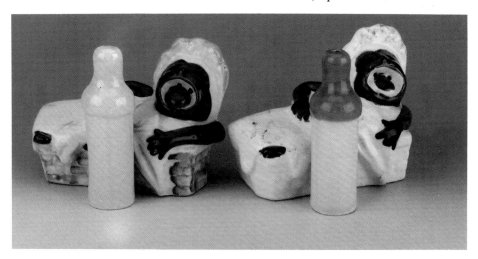

Crying babies in basket with bottles. 3". Probably Japan. Early 1950s. $100-125.

Girls (perhaps singles). 1.75". Germany . Pre-WWII. $65-75 each.

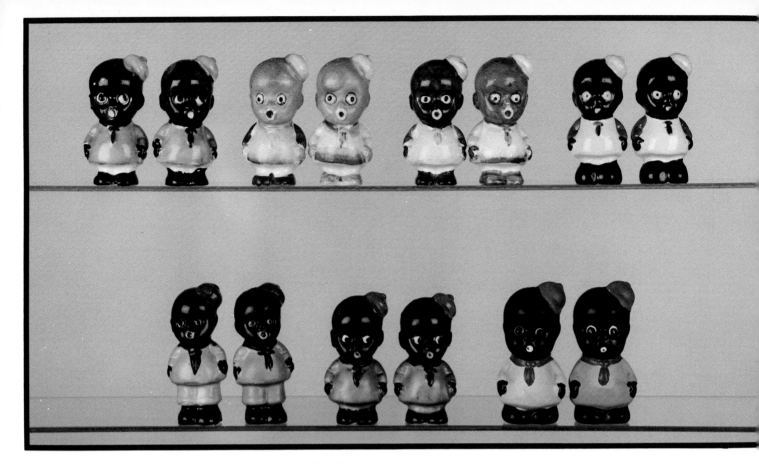

"Snowflake". 3.25". All sets except last set on second row, Japan.
Pre-1950. $50-55. Last set on second row, reproduction. Taiwan.
1990s. $10-12.

Senior citizens. 4.5". Maker unknown, "877 USA" incised on bottom.
1960s. $90-100.

Face condiment. 4.5" wide. Germany. Pre-WWII. One eye is pepper, other eye is mustard lid. $250+.

Children taking Saturday night baths. 2.75". Japan. Early 1950s. $150-175.

Man gesturing to woman. 3.25". Probably U.S.A. 1960s. $75-85.

Children holding bananas. 2.5". Maker unknown. 1970s. If in good condition, $40-50.

Angel head stacker. 3.25". Probably U.S.A. 1960s. $55-65.

Black head and gloves, "The Al Jolson Set". 2.5". Probably U.S.A. 1960s. $125-150.

Natives with alligator and dish. 2.25". Maker unknown. 1960s or later. $75-85.

Nodder, royalty in Viking ship. Red mustard top missing. 3.5". Japan.
1950s. Apparently marketed primarily in New Zealand and Australia.
If complete, $250+.

"Ethiopian Guards". Center set, 4.75". Ceramic Arts Studio,
Madison, WI. 1950s. $115-125. Left and right sets, 4" and 3".
Occupied Japan, late 1940s. $45-50.

Genie or palace guard? 6.5". Paper label, "Elvin,
handpainted, Japan." 1960s. Mate unknown to authors;
can you identify his mate? Single, $50-60.

People wearing turbans. First row, 2.75"-3.5". Germany. Pre-WWII.
Sets, $65-75. Singles, $25. Second row, 3.25". First and second sets,
chalkware. U.S.A. 1950s. $20-25. Third set, Japan. Pre-1950. $40-45.

People with turbans. 4". Goebel, Germany, mold
no. P386. $150-175.

Couples with turbans. 3.5". Japan. 1950s. $45-50.

Man with turban, lady with water jug. 4.25". Japan. Pre-1950. $75-85.

People with turbans. 3". Marked "Wyn, Carmel" (CA). Probably 1950s. $100-125.

Genies. 4". Private ceramicist. U.S.A. 1970s. $50-60.

"Mammys Salt and Pepper". 3". Japan. Pre-1950. $65-75.

Men with turbans. 3". Germany. Mold #7219. Pre-WWII. $90-100.

Black Sambo and the tiger, by Ceramic Arts Studio. Black Sambo is
3.5", tiger is 5.25" long. 1950s. $500+.

Singers with palm tree. 4.25". Japan. 1960s. $100-125.

Royalty? 3.25". Japan. 1960s. $50-60.

"Basket weaver, Charleston, SC". 4.25". Japan. 1980s. $35-40.

Ladies with fruit baskets. 4". Probably Japan. 1960s. $75-85.

Watermelon nodders. 3.5". Japan. 1950s. Note teeth in first set, no teeth in second set. Fifth nodder is brown pottery . $200-250.

Brown watermelon nodder with teeth.

Boy and girl eating watermelons. Boy , 4.5". Girl, 5". Paper label, Japan. 1960s. $90-100.

Men holding watermelons with variations in size and clothing. 5"-3.75". Japan. 1950s. First and second sets, $175-200. Third set, $160-175. Fourth set, $140-150. Fifth set, $90-100.

Boy holding leaf trays with watermelons. 3". Japan. Pre-1950. $100-125.

Chef holding trays with watermelon slices. 4.25". Japan. Pre-1950. $125-140.

Children with watermelon slices. 4.5". Japan. 1960s. $200-250.

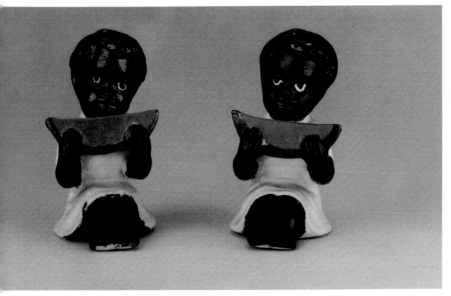

Children eating watermelon. Bisque finish. 2.25". Japan. $75-90.

Man eating watermelon. 4.75". 1950s. $150-175.

Heads with watermelon slices. 2.5". Left set, probably U.S.A. 1970s. Right set, Japan. 1960s. $50-60.

Girl with watermelon slice in lap. 2.75". Probably U.S.A. 1970s. $75-90.

Native eating watermelon. 3.5". Japan. 1960s. $90-100.

Native holding watermelon slice. 2.5". Japan. 1950s. $90-100.

Kissing natives on benches. 4.5". Paper label, Japan. 1960s. Left set, $110-125. Center and right sets, $65-75.

Ladies heads with upturned hat brims. First row: first set, 2.25". Japan. 1950s. $55-60. Second and third sets with watermelons, 2.25". Probably U.S.A. 1960s. If in good condition, $40-45. Second row: Children with watermelons. 4". Probably U.S.A. 1960s. $90-100.

Boy holding watermelon slice, and slice of watermelon. 2.5". Japan. Pre-1950. $100-125.

People with watermelons. First row: first set, chalkware. 2.5". U.S.A. 1950s. $75-85. Second set, 2.25". Gale Gerds of Wisconsin. 1990s. $30-35. Second row: first set, 2". Japan. Pre-1950. $90-100. Second set, 2". Gale Gerds. 1990s. $25-30.

Stacking native heads. 4.5". Paper label, Japan. 1960s. $110-125.

Native boy and girl riding goat; they fit into a depression in the back of the goat. 4.75". Japan. Pre-1950. $250+.

Native couple. 3". Japan. Pre-1950. $75-85.

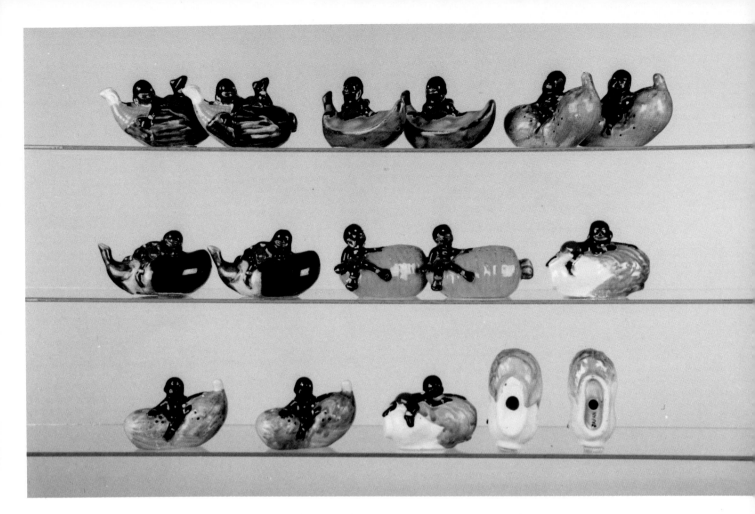

Native boys riding vegetables. First and second rows depict original Japan sets. 2.25". $90-100. Sets on bottom row are reproductions. 1990s. $15-20. To identify difference, examine area surrounding cork hole. Original set is painted the color of the vegetable and is glazed. Reproduction set is not painted but may be lightly glazed.

Native condiment, face is mustard, tongue is spoon. 3" high, 6.5" long. Japan. 1960s. $250-300.

Natives on tray with hut condiment. 3". Japan. 1960s. $100-110.

Natives with pink trim. $80-90.

Native with cooking pot. 3". Paper label, Japan. 1960s. $90-100.
Native hanging from tree. 4". Marked foreign (probably Japan).
1960s. $125-150.

Natives. 2"-3". Japan. 1960s. Pink trimmed set, $80-90. Others, $60-70.

Natives. 2.5"-3". Japan. 1960s. $75-85.

Natives with alligators. First row, 4". Japan. 1960s. $90-100. Second row: first and second sets, 4". Japan. 1950s. $110-125. Third set, 3.25". Paper label, Japan. 1960s. $75-85.

Native couples. 4". Japan. 1960s. $40-50.

Natives with hut condiment. 6.25". Royal, Handpainted, Japan. 1960s. $200-250.

Natives 2.5". Japan. 1960s. $85-95.

Natives. Left, 4.5". Right, 5.5". Japan, 1960s. $85-95.

Resting native children. 2.5". Probably Japan. 1960s. $65-75.

Native with bone resting on top of head. 4.25". No mark, probably
U.S.A. 1960s. $100-110.

Natives on drums. 5.75". Japan. 1960s. $75-85.

Native heads with bone jewelry. 3.25". Probably U.S.A. 1970s. $60-
75.

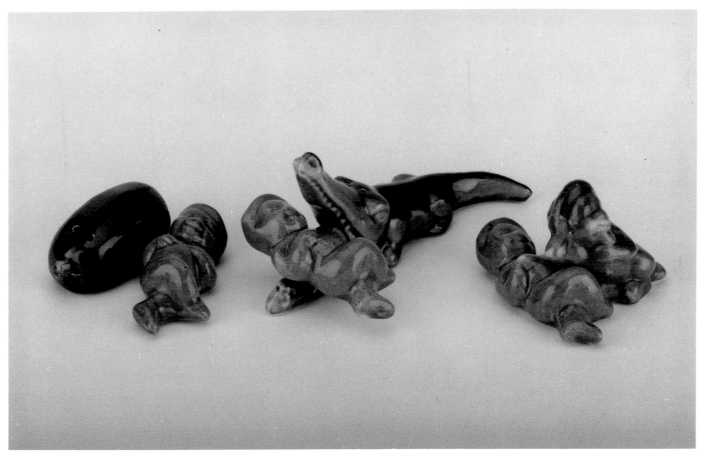

Boy with blue hat brim paired with three different pieces. Boy in alligator's mouth: gator is 5.25" long, 2.5" high. Boy and brother with red hat brim, 1.5". Boy with watermelon, 1". U.S.A., 1960s, $90-100.

Native. 3". Japan. 1960s. Can you identify his mate? Single, $30-35.

Graduates. 3.25". Japan. 1950s. $90-100.

Native with explorer in pot. 1.75". Arcadia Ceramics, CA. 1950s.
$80-90.

"How to Serve your Fellow Man". Native reading
cookbook, explorer in pot. Paper label, Japan.
1960s. $125-140.

Native with pot and hut. 2.5". Probably U.S.A.
1960s. $90-100.

Native family waiting for dinner. 5.5". Paper label, Japan. 1960s. Tall
set with mustard, $175-200. Small set, $75-85.

Musicians. Set on left: 3.5". Probably Japan. 1950s. Copy of set at right. $75-100. Set on right: 3.5". Goebel, mold no. P111A&B. 1950s. $125-150.

Hugging, kissing natives. 3.25". Goebel, Germany, mold no. P92A&B. 1950s. $150-175.

Kissing natives. 3". Japan. 1960s. $35-40.

Natives with bongo drums, gold trim. 3". Probably U.S.A. 1960s. $50-60.

Natives riding alligators and hippo. First row playing banjos, 3.25"-3.5". Japan. 1950s. $75-85. Second row: first set, 3". Ceramic Arts Studio. 1950s. $150-175. Second set, 3.75". Japan. 1950s. $150-175. Third set, 3". Japan. 1960s. $90-100. Third row, 3"-3.5". Japan. 1950s. $75, $100, $125.

Native mom carrying child on platform formed by her arms. 6". Probably Japan. 1960s. If in good condition, $75-85.

Native moms holding babies. 4.75". Japan. 1950s. More common left set: $45-50. Right set: $75-85.

Native chieftains with headdress. 3.25". Japan. 1950s. $45-55.

Arab boy sitting on camel. Total height, 4.75". Japan. 1950s. Left set, $200-225. Right set with brown camel, rare, $250-275.

Jonah and the Whale. Boy sits on knob on whale's back. Total height, 3.5". Japan. 1960s. $100-125.

Natives riding elephants. 5.5". First and third sets, Japan. Center set, Ceramic Arts Studio. Note difference in direction of elephant's trunk and boy's arm on third set. First and third sets, $125-150. Center set, $175-200.

Native heads with gold jewelry. 4.25". Probably U.S.A. 1960s. Note: the center set has white eyes; the right set has gold eyes. Left and center sets, $35-40. Right set, $45-50.

Natives with baskets on heads and bones through hair. 3"-4". Japan. 1960s. Tall set, $45-50. Green baskets, $55-60. Small set, $35-40.

Native with shields. 2.75". Set on left, Japan. 1950s. $55-65. Set on right is reproduction, distributed by Sarsaparilla Deco Designs, NJ. 1980s. $20-25.

Native girl and hut. One of a series of international people with objects. 4.5". Japan. 1950s. $85-100.

Boy matador and bull. 3.5". Composition material. Probably Japan. 1970s. $50-60.

Matador and bull. 4". Paper label, Japan. 1970s. $55-65.

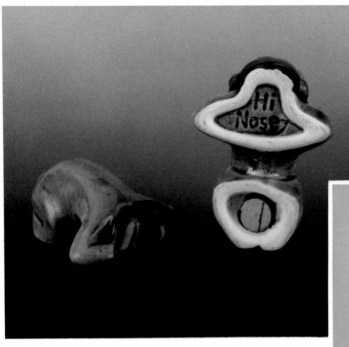

"Hi Nosey". 1.5". U.S.A. 1960s. $65-75.

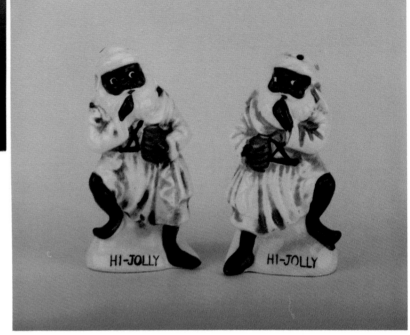

"Hi-Jolly". 3". Japan. 1950s. He was an Arab camel driver in Arizona in mid-1800s. $75-85.

Boys playing leap frog. 3.75". Japan. Pre-1950. $85-95.

Native heads, ceramic with wooden bodies. 5.25". Japan. 1950s. $85-100.

Native heads on pots. 5.5". Paper label, Japan. 1960s. If in good condition, $90-100.

Natives with baskets. 4.75". Set on left, Japan. 1950s. $50-60. Set on right, probably U.S.A. 1960s. $75-85.

Native playing banjo under palm tree. 3". Japan. 1950s. $40-50.

Native heads with metal earrings. 6". Nasco, Japan. 1960s. $45-50.

Couple with real metal earrings. 3.5". Japan. $65-75.

Native with large lips. 4". Private ceramicist. U.S.A. 1970s. $35-40.

Native couples with metal earrings and blinking eyes. 4.25". Brinnco, Japan. 1960s. $45-50.

Native heads with neckbands. 3.5". Probably U.S.A. 1960s. Set $35-40, single $15-18.

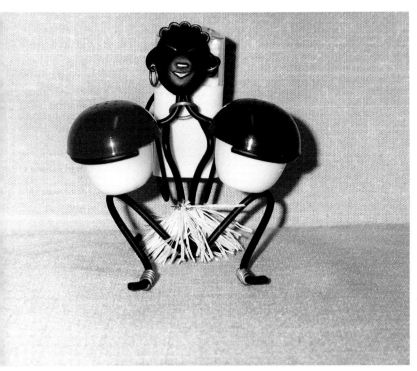

Island bongo player, metal frame, plastic shakers, paper skirt. 5". Japan. 1960s. $60-65.

Island bongo player. Metal frame, wooden head, ceramic shakers, paper skirt. 5.5". Japan. 1960s. $55-60.

Triangles, ceramic. 3.25". Sonsco, Japan. 1970s. $60-70.

Brazilian musician and dancer. 2.75". Zitrin, Brazil. 1970s. $50-60.

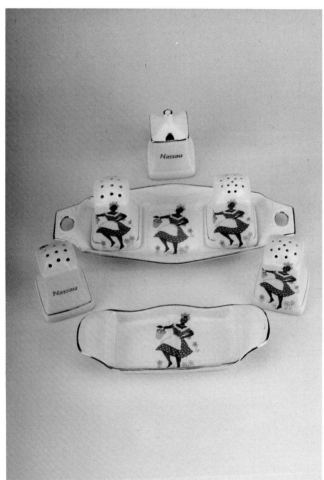

Nassau sets. 2.75". Royal Winton, England. 1970s. S&P $50-60. Condiment $75-85.

Natives. 3". Possibly Brazil. 1970s. $50-60.

"Sublime Point, N.S.W." Aborigine children, New South Wales, Australia. 3". Maker unknown. 1960s. $65-75.

Nudes. Left to right: 5.75", 5.25", 5.75". First two, Paper label, Japan; right set, U.S.A. 1960s/1970s. First two: $75-85, right set: $40-50.

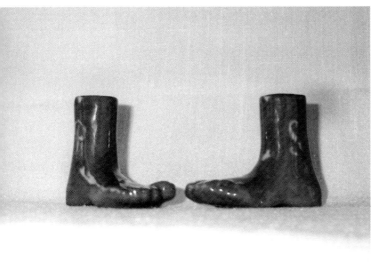

Brown feet. 2". No mark. Private ceramicist. U.S.A. 1970s. $25-30.

Black feet. Length, 3.25". Probably U.S.A. 1960s. $30-35.

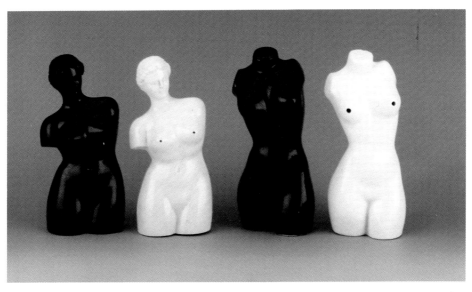

Venus de Milo. 4". U.S.A. 1970s. Set on left is plastic. $15-18. Set on right is ceramic, $25-30.

Lady with flower basket s. 3". Japan. 1960s. $90-100. Right set, children with real cloth covers. 4". Probably Japan. 1960s. $110-125.

Lady in rocking chair. 4". Japan. 1960s. $75-85.

Man with burger. 2.75". Possibly U.S.A. 1960s. $55-65.

"Smokquee, The Royal, Boise, Idaho", advertising chefs. 3". Japan. 1950s. $200-225.

Children shooting dice; dice are attached to tray . 3". Japan. Pre-1950. Paint consistently poor on all sets seen. $125-140.

Singer and piano. 4". No mark, probably U.S.A. 1960s. $100-125.

Porter and suitcase. 2.75". Distributed by Parkcraft, Burlington, IA. 1950s. $90-100.

"Porgy and Bess". 5.25". Copyrighted 1950, Reebs, USA. $150-175.

Man with removable bottles in pockets. 6.25". Germany . 1960s. $125-150.

Porter carrying suitcases. 4.5". Japan. Pre-1950. Note: shaker on left has larger holes. Shakers sometimes marked S&P . $225-250.

Shoe shine boy and box. 3". Japan. 1960s. $125-150.

Boys sitting on cotton bales. Left set, 4.5". Japan. 1960s. $125-150.
Right set, 3.5". Possibly Parkcraft, based on bottom of bale. 1960s.
$100-125.

Couple. 3.75". Brown County Pottery, Nashville, IN. 1960s/1970s.
$100-125.

Courting couple. 3.5". Maker unknown. 1980s. $50-70.

Children. 2.5". What do these fit in? No marks. Unable to price.

Golliwogs. First row, 3.75". Silver Crane Company, England. 1980s.
$225-250. Second row, golliwogs leaning on balls. 3". Probably
Japan. 1950s. $150-175. (*Note:* First 2 sets mismatched).

Captain and mate. 5.25". Grimes, California. 1960s. $125-150.

Seal trainer and seal. 3.5". Japan. 1960s. $95-110.

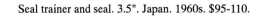

Boy with crest of Torrington, England. 3.75". England. Early 1900s.
Rare. $250+.

73

Children in baskets. 3.5". Japan. 1950s/1960s. First and third rows, all sets, $90-100. Second row, $125-150.

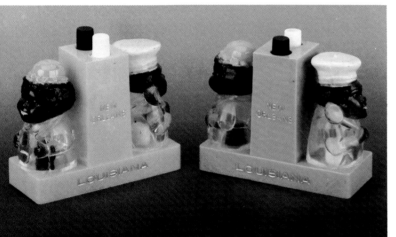

One-piece push buttons. 2.75". Hong Kong. 1970s/80s. Made in several colors. $50-60.

Men on toilets. 5.1"-4". Japan. Pre-1950. Sets arranged in descending order of size. Some toilets white with blue and yellow trim. Others, white with brown trim. If in good condition, $75-100.

Aunt Jemima and Uncle Mose. First row: 5", 5.5", 3.5". F&F Mold and Dye Works, Dayton, OH. 1950s. First set, $65-75. Syrup, $60-65. Third set, $45-50. Second row, reproductions. 5". First set, unmarked. Probably 1960s. Original mold apparently used to make this set. $40-45. Set on right marked "Miss Martha Originals, Inc. Antique Repro". U.S.A. 1980s. $20-25. Third row, ceramic reproductions. Taiwan. 1980s. $10-15.

"Langniappe of New Orleans" Tea Company. 5.25". F & F Mold and Dye Works, Dayton, OH. 1950s. $175-200.

Luzianne Coffee of New Orleans. Set on left made by Carol Gifford of Oklahoma. 5". 1990s. $50-60. Set on right: F & F Mold and Dye Works, Dayton, OH. 1950s. $200-225, mint. Unpainted single, 4.5". Probably U.S.A. 1960s. $75-85.

Heads with handles (ladies missing handles). 3"-3.5". Paper label, Japan. 1960s. If complete, ladies $150-175. Santa teapots and firemen, $60-65.

Clown holding salt and pepper, oil and vinegar. 8.25". Thames, Japan. 1960s. $75-85.

Clown holding one-piece accordion S&P. 6". Japan. 1960s. $110-125.

Clown face teapots. 4". Paper label, Japan. 1960s. $45-50.

Island band members. 5". Paper label, Japan. 1970s. $65-75.

Clown face wall pocket with hanging spices. 8.25". Paper label, Japan. 1960s. $75-85.

Couples, composition. 3". Probably U.S.A. 1950s. If in good condition, $50-60.

Sitting maids, composition. 3.5". Probably U.S.A. 1950s. $40-45.

"Before" & "After". Chalkware. 1.25". U.S.A. Early 1950s. $90-100.

Native heads with gold neckbands. Chalkware. 2.5". U.S.A. 1950s. $45-50.

Chefs and maids. First row, chalkware. 2.5". U.S.A. 1950s. Set $45-50, single $20-25. Second row, 2.5". First and second sets, probably U.S.A. 1960s. $40-45. Third set, Japan. 1950s. $45-50.

Chalkware senior citizens. 2.75". U.S.A. 1950s. If in good condition, set $50-60; single, $20-25.

Wooden people. 6". No mark. Probably Japan. 1970s. $22-25.

Wooden, island scene and coffee server. 3.75". Maker unknown.
1950s. $22-25.

"Rastus and Liza". Wooden. 3". Japan. 1960s. $25-28.

"I'se From Lewis Plantation". Wooden with decal. 2.25". Probably
Japan. 1940s. $65-75.

Wooden chefs. 3"-3.5". Japan. 1960s. $12-15.

Wooden chefs. 2-5". Japan. 1960s. Large $22-25, medium $12-15, small $8-10.

Wooden Island policeman with metal earrings. 4". Japan. 1970s. $18-20.

Various wooden sets. 2"-7". Japan. 1950s/1960s. $5-25.

Wooden native and rhino. 2.5". Maker unknown. 1960s. $20-25.

Wooden natives with metal jewelry. 4" and 3.5". Japan. 1960s. Large $22-25, others $18-20.

"Rio Rita". 4". Taiwan. 1980s. Fitz & Floyd, TX. Discontinued by company. Issue price $20, current value $75-85.

"Mandy" children. 2.75". Japan. 1980s. Omnibus Division of Fitz & Floyd, Discontinued by company. Issue price $20, current value $45-50.

"African-American Santa". 4.5". Taiwan. 1993. Omnibus Division of Fitz & Floyd. $15-18.

Boxers. 3.25". Korea. 1990s. Sarsaparilla Deco Designs. $15-18.

"The Jazz Set". 6". U.S.A. Sculptural Ceramics, WA. 1990s. $35-40.

"Someone's Kitchen". 4". Japan. 1980s. Department 56, MN. $25-30.

Sets on this and the following two pages were designed and produced by pottery artist Rick Wisecarver of Ohio in the 1990's

"Afloat on the Mississippi". 3-piece set produced for the 1990 S&P Club Convention. Shown is the #1 set. 5". One of 600 sets produced. Sold at the Convention Auction for $450. Regular set originally sold for $25. Current value $75-100.

Gone with the Wind". Designed and produced by Rick Wisecarver as the alternate 1990 Convention set. This #1 Set on left is one-of-a-kind.

Set produced for commercial sale. 4". 1990. Issue price $40, current value $75-85.

"Cotton Pickers" condiment. 4". $60-70.

Mammy and Pappy heads. 3.5". $50-60.

Angels. 3.75". $40-50.

"Watermelon Children". 5.25". $50-60.

"Country Couple". 4.25". $50-60.

"Grandpa Washington". 5.75". Jerry P. Miller, KS. 1993. $45-50.

"Sister Ruth". 6". Jerry P. Miller,. 1993. $45-50.

"Porsha". 6.5". Jerry P. Miller. 1993. $50.

Cat Characters

Tom heads. 2". Japan. 1960s. $90-100.

Tom and Jerry. 3". Marked foreign (probably Japan). 1960s. Rare. $200+.

Hello Kitty. 2.75". Paper label, Japan. 1980. Gold sticker on back with name. © 1976 by Sanrio Surprises, distributed by Sanrio Co. Ltd. $85-100.

Pink Panther. 3.5". Probably Japan. ©1983 United Artists. $200-225.

"Felix Keeps on Walking". 2.5". Germany. 1920s. Four digit number on bottom. Extremely rare. Sold at 'Tiques Auction in 1992 for $1100.

Felix. 3". Japan. 1940s. Movable eyes. Sold at Tiques Auction, 1994. $400+.

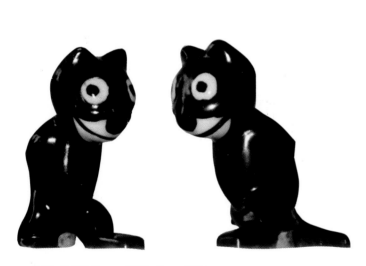

Felix. 2.25". Japan. 1950s. Rare. $400+.

Felix. 3.5". Probably Taiwan. 1994. Prototype S&P shown with cookie jar. Issued by Benjamin and Medwin, Inc., NY. $12-15.

Gold Felix. 4". Japan. 1950s. Rare. $400+.

Felix, front and side views. 3". Japan. Rare. 1950s. $400+.

Si and Am. 3.5". Paper label, Japan. 1950s. Unlicensed, from
Disney's Lady and the Tramp. 6 poses shown. $100-125.

Kliban in red boots, composition material. 2". No mark. 1970s. $125-150.

Kliban emerging from egg. 3.75". Japan. 1970s. Designed by B. Kliban and issued by Sigma, the Taste Setter. $200-225.

Kliban with victrola. 3.25". Japan. 1970s. Designed by B. Kliban and issued by Sigma. $200-225.

Sylvester. 4". Japan. 1970s. Licensed by Warner Bros., distributed by Enterprise Sales and Distributors Ltd., Toronto, Canada. $150-175.

Sylvester and Tweety. Left set, 3". Right set, 4.5". Licensed by Warner Brothers. Taiwan. 1992/1989. $25-30.

Sylvester and Tweety. Paper decals on glass with metal tops. 4". Licensed by Warner Brothers. Canada. 1993. $8-10.

Sylvester. 4.5". China. 1993. Prototype, not issued by Certified
International Corp. (CIC), NY. $75-100.

Sylvester and Tweety. 4.5". China. 1993. Set issued by CIC. Different
from prototype in eyes, whiskers and bottom. $15-18.

Figaro on basket. 4". Goebel, Germany. 1950s. Licensed by Walt Disney Productions. Mold number DIS 138A&B. Rare. $400+.

Figaro. Set on left, 3.5". Set on right, 2.75". Japan. 1960s. $65-75.

Figaro. 4.25". American Bisque Co., U.S.A. 1960s. $225-250.

Figaro. 4". No mark, flat unglazed bottom, probably U.S.A. 1960s. $100-125.

Figaro. 3". National Porcelain Co., Trenton, NJ. 1941-42. ©WDP faintly incised on back. Produced in the four colors shown. $75-85.

"Figaro and Cleo". 2.75". Unlicensed U.S.A. 1960s. $65-75.

Figaro. 3". Probably USA. 1940s. $55-65.

All Garfield S&Ps were licensed by United Features Syndicate, Inc.
©1978 and 1981. All but one set were issued by the Enesco Corp. of
Illinois.

Garfield and Arlene. 3". Korea. 1989. $55-65.

Santa Garfield heads. 3". China 1993. $15-18.

Garfield and Arlene. 4". Japan. 1980s. Figurines, not S&P. A wedding
S&P was advertised in the mid-1980s by The Ferry House, a mail
order company from Iowa. The company went out of business about
the same time period. Does anyone have the S&P? We are assuming
it's similar to this illustration.

Santa Garfield heads. 4". Probably Japan. 1980s. $100-125.

"Halloween Garfield". 2.5". Taiwan. 1989. $20-25.

Garfield "Loose in the Kitchen". 3.5".
Taiwan. 1990. Issued by Molly Houseware
Ltd., England. $50-60.

Chef Garfield and Garfield emerging from egg. Left set, 4". Japan.
Right set, 3.25". Taiwan. 1980s. $90-100.

Garfield and Odie. 4". Taiwan. 1980s. $65-75.

Niagara Falls

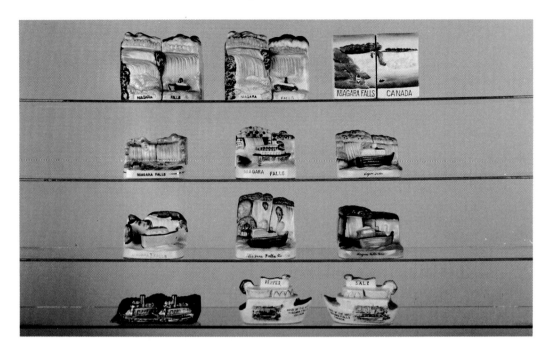

Niagara Falls Maid of the Mist. First row , 3.25". Two pieces fit together to form scene. Japan. 1950s. First and second sets, $15-18. Third set, $25-30. Second and third rows, three-piece sets, 2.25"-3". First set, both falls are shakers. Remaining sets, falls is one shaker and boat is other. Japan. 1950s/1960s. $25-30. Fourth row, 1.5"-2.25". Japan. 1950s/1960s. First set, $22-25. Second set, $12-15.

Niagara Falls. First row, 3"-3.5". First and third sets, Germany . Center, U.S.A. $40-45. Second row, 3". First and fourth sets, Germany. Second and third sets, Czechoslovakia. Pre-WWII. $22-25. Third row, antique milk glass with metal tops. 3.75". U.S.A., Pre-WWII. $50-65.

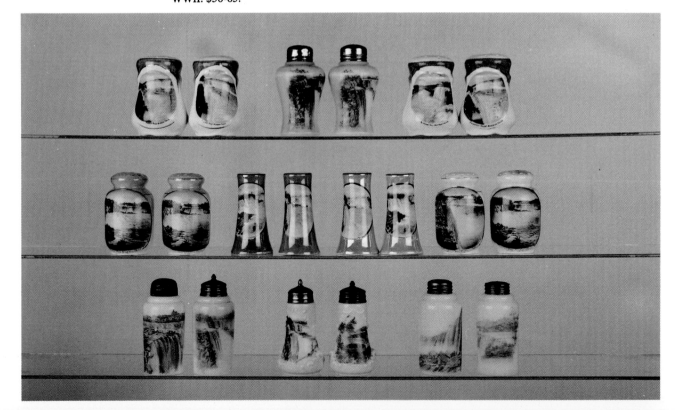

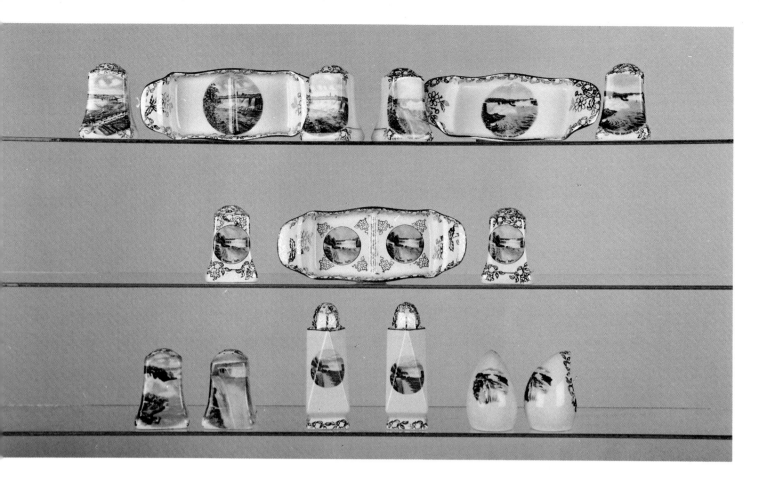

Niagara Falls. All sets made by Royal Winton, England. 1950s. First and second rows, 3". Three-piece sets, different scenes. $25-30. Third row, 3"-4". First and third sets probably originally sold with a tray. Priced without tray, $15-18. Center set, $20-25.

Niagara Falls condiments. First row, 2.5". Germany. Pre-WWII. $50-60. Second row, 3". Japan. 1950s. $25-30. Third row, 3". Japan. 1950s/1960s. First and second sets, $20-25, third set, $12-15.

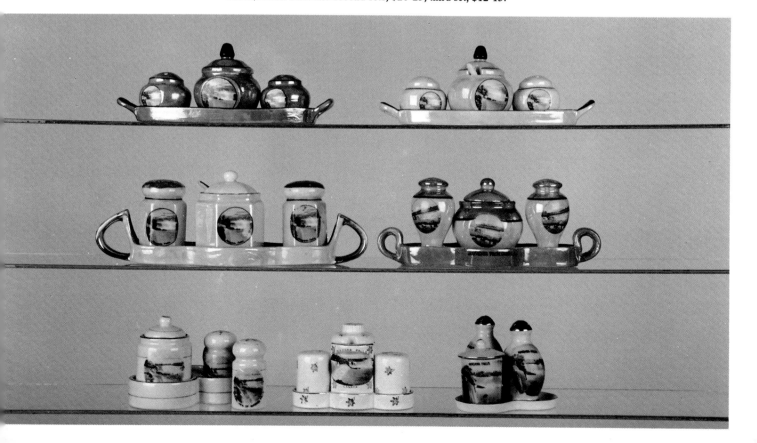

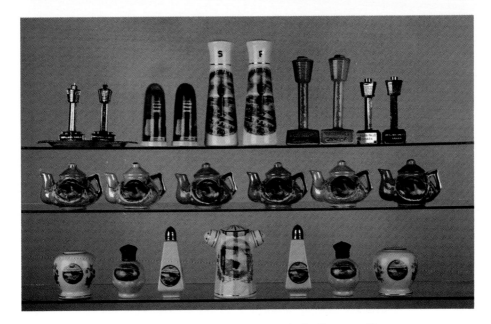

Niagara Falls. First row, 3.75-5.5". All sets depict Seagrams Tower. Snow domes made in Hong Kong. All others, Japan. 1970s. First and last sets, $8-10. Snow domes, $18-20. Center set, $12-15. Gray ceramic set, $15-18. Second row, Moriage teapots. 2.25". Paper label, Japan. 1960s. $15-18. Third row, 2.25"-3.5". Japan. 1950s/1960s. Center one-piece shaker, $30-35. Other sets, $8-10.

Niagara Falls. First row, 2.5"-3.5". First two singles, Germany. Pre-WWII. $25-30. Center set, Austria. Pre-WWII. $50-60. Third set, Germany. Pre-WWII. $50-60. Second row, 2.5"-4.25". First set, Czechoslovakia. Pre-WWII. $40-45. Second set, chef and maid, U.S.A. 1950s. $60-70. Third set, Italy. 1970s. $12-15. Third row, 1.5"-4". First and third sets, possibly Japan. 1950s. $8-10. Center set, Japan. 1950s. If in good condition, $25-30.

Niagara Falls. First row, 4.75"-5.75". First set probably U.S.A.
Others, Japan. 1950s/1960s. First set, $15-20. Others, $8-10. Second
row, 2.5". Possibly U.S.A. 1950s. $22-25. Third row, 3.5"-4.25".
Japan. Pre-1950. First and third sets, $12-15. Center condiment, $40-
45.

Niagara Falls. First row, 3.75". Japan. Pre-1950. $15-18. Second row:
condiments, 3". Japan. 1950s. $20-25. Third row, 2"-4". First set,
Noritake, Japan. 1950s. $60-75. Second set, Bavaria, Germany . Pre-
WWII. $60-75. Third set, Japan. 1950s. $25-30.

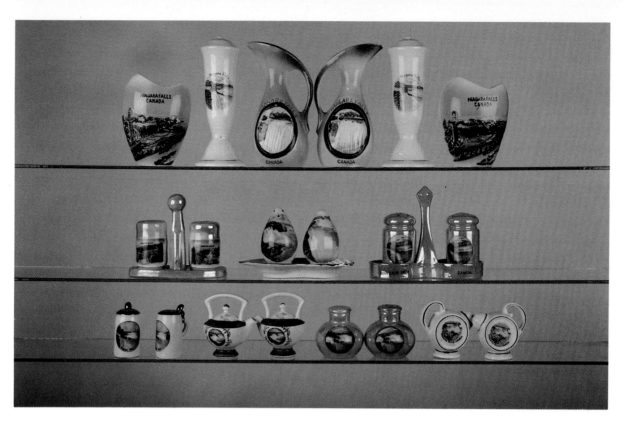

Niagara Falls. First row, 4"-5". Brown and white set, U.S.A. Others, Japan. 1960s. U.S.A. set, $15-20. Others, $8-10. Second row , 3"-4". First set, Germany. Pre-WWII. $40-45. Second set, Royal Winton, England. 1950s. $25-30. Third set, Japan. 1960s. $25-30. Third row, 2"-2.5". Steins, Germany. 1950s. $15-18. Tea kettles, Japan. 1960s. $10-12. Lustre, Czechoslovakia. 1950s. $15-18. White kettles, Japan. 1960s. $8-10.

Niagara Falls. First and second rows, all Moriage. 3". Japan. 1960s. $15-18. Third row, 3". Paper label, Japan. 1960s. $10-12.

Mermaids

Black mermaids. 3". Japan. 1950s. $200-250.

Deep sea diver and mermaid. 3". U.S.A. 1960s. $45-50.

Deep sea diver and mermaid. 3.5". Probably U.S.A. 1960s. $55-65.

Mermaids. First row, holding shells. 3", 3.5", 3.75". Japan. 1960s.
Left set, $35-40. Single (marked sample), $25. Right set, $40-45.
Second row: 2.5", 3.5", 3.5". Japan. 1960s. $40-45, $25-30, $25-30.
Third row: 3.25", 3", 2.5". First set, probably Taiwan. 1980s. $12-15.
Second set, paper label, Japan. 1970s. $45-50. Third set, Fitz &
Floyd. Japan. 1981. $50-55.

Mermaid and treasure chest condiment. 2". Sandy Srp. 1992. One of
only three sets produced. Real semi-precious stones in chest. $1150 at
the 1992 S&P Club Convention Auction.

Mermaids. First row: 3", 4.5", 2.75". Jean Grief, CA. 1990s. $12-15. Second row, mermaids and mermen. 3"-3.25". First two sets, Japan. Pre-1950. $15-18. Third and fourth sets: Miyao, Japan, Napco Import. 1960s. $25-35. Third row: 3.5", 1.75", 3.75". Japan. 1950s/ 1960s. First and third sets, $35-40. Center set, $45-50.

Mermaid. 2.75". Miyao, Japan. 1960s. "Long time No She" and "Long Time No He." $25-35.

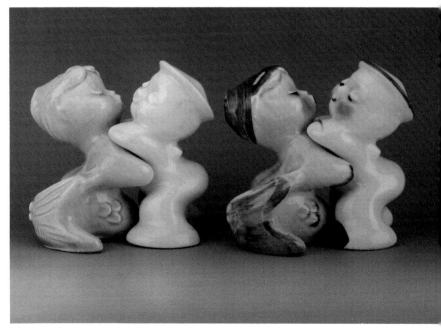

Van Tellingen sailor and mermaid. Set on left is unpainted version of set on right. 4". Regal China Corp., IL. 1960s. $175-200.

Mermaids. First row: 4", 4.25", 3.75". Paper label, Japan. 1960s. $45-50, $25-30, $30-35. Second row: 4.25", 3.5", 2.75". First set, Quon-Quon, Japan. Second set, Clay Art, Philippines. Third set, paper label, Japan. 1980s/1990s. $45-50, $18-20, $10-12. Third row, mermaids with starfish. 2". Probably U.S.A. 1960s. $45-50.

Sailor and mermaid. 5.75". G Novelty Co. Japan. 1960s. $65-75.

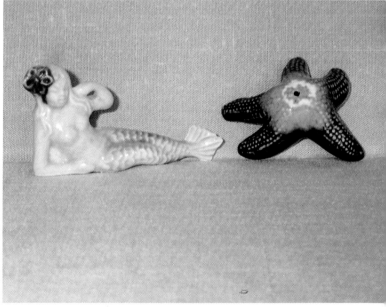

Mermaid with starfish. 2". Probably USA. 1960s. $45-50.

Crested and souvenirs. First row: first piece, 2.5". W.H. Goss, England. Early 1900s. Crest of Ostende, Belgium. $50. Three-piece set, 2.75". Czechoslovakia. 1920s. Crest of Liverpool, England. $40. Third piece, 2.5". W.H. Goss, England. Early 1900s. Crest of Lytham, England. $50. Second and third rows, "The Lorelei". Copenhagen, Denmark. 2"-3". Small sets possibly Denmark. Tall sets, Japan. 1970s. $12-15.

Snow domes, from Weeki Wachee, FL. 3.25". Hong Kong. 1960s/1970s. $12-15.

Mermaid stacker. 5". Japan. 1950s. Separates at waist. $75-85.

"Deep Sea Cats". 3.25". Clay Art. Philippines. 1991. $15-18.

"Fisherman's Dream". 4.75". Sculptural Ceramics, WA. 1990s. $35-40.

Mermaid and fish. Set on left is prototype, set on right is the final version. 4". Philippines. Issued by Strata Group, NY. 1992. $15-18.